GROWING OLD DOESN'T MEAN GROWING UP

Clive Whichelow
and Mike Haskins

summersdale

GROWING OLD DOESN'T MEAN GROWING UP

An Hachette UK Company
www.hachette.co.uk

Summersdale Publishers Ltd
Part of Octopus Publishing Group Limited
Carmelite House
50 Victoria Embankment
LONDON
EC4Y 0DZ
UK

www.summersdale.com

Printed and bound in China

ISBN: 978-1-80007-403-3

INTRODUCTION

So, you're a little bit older. You're a mature, respected grown-up. But there's just one problem. Being grown up sometimes doesn't seem that much fun. There are endless bills to pay. Work. Jobs. Chores. Problems. And that's before we even get on to the people you have to deal with! It was all so much simpler back in the good old days when you were young, immature and perhaps even slightly stupid. Life was a lot more enjoyable when you didn't have any responsibilities.

But there's good news. Just because you're a little bit older, it doesn't mean you have to start acting old. The universe is over 13 billion years old, so you're probably nowhere near that yet – well, not quite anyway. The universe doesn't go around moaning about being old, does it? No, it just gets on with it. You don't hear the universe complaining about aching joints and people speaking too quietly, do you?

It's never too early to start enjoying your second childhood, to stop taking life too seriously and to start acting a bit silly again. So, come on! Snap out of it! And let's make the most of life! Or if we can't always do that, let's at least have a good old laugh while trying.

After all, as a wise man once said: growing old doesn't mean growing up!

TELL-TALE SIGNS YOU'RE GETTING OLDER BUT DON'T WANT TO BE GROWN UP

You wear sensible shoes –
but very silly socks

You insist your birthday cake has
the full number of candles required
for your age, even at the risk of
incinerating your own home

You like to snuggle up each night with
your childhood teddy bear – no matter
what your partner thinks about it

You take great pride in your garden, but your lawnmower also has go-faster stripes

THINGS TO WORRY ABOUT FOR GROWN-UPS AND NOT-GROWN-UPS

GROWN-UPS	NOT-GROWN-UPS
Will my pension cover my food bills?	Will my pension cover my alcohol bills?
Who should I put as beneficiaries in my will?	How can I blow the lot before anyone else gets their hands on it?
How many years until I can retire?	How many years until I can tell my boss exactly what I think of them?
Should I be paying more attention to my health?	How much can I get away with before my health notices?

REASONS MATURITY IS OVERRATED

It's just a polite way of saying "old"

Because unless you're a cheese or a wine,
it's hard to see anything good about it

Acquiring the wisdom of years is a bit
pointless if no one wants to listen to you

Mature pursuits like opera
and literature are all very well
but they will never bring as
much joy as a carefully
placed whoopee cushion

CHILDISH HOBBIES YOU CAN TAKE UP AGAIN AND THE EXCUSES YOU CAN GIVE FOR THEM

Playing with toy cars – it's safer than driving a real one at your age

Dressing up as your favourite superhero – you're on a mission to deter criminals by making them laugh so much at the sight of you

Painting – you can now claim your doodles are primitivist artworks worth millions

THINGS YOU SHOULD NEVER STOP DOING

Drawing pictures on steamed-up windows

Shouting in a tunnel to see if it echoes

Avoiding stepping on the cracks in
the pavement – as well as being a fun
game, it helps you avoid any
filthy puddles underfoot

Singing happily at the top of your voice without embarrassment (at least not to yourself)

HOW THE YOUNG ARE CATCHING UP WITH THE OLD

OLD	YOUNG
Mobility scooters	Electric scooters
React-to-light spectacles	Shades
Supports and replacement body parts to try to hold you together	Piercings
Having a social life, talking to people, making friends, occasionally establishing lifelong relationships	Texting

WAYS TO RESIST BEING GROWN UP

Hang a stocking up at Christmas
(even though it may still be empty
on Christmas morning)

Practise doing wheelies while
using your exercise bike

Skip happily along wherever you
go – whether you're on the way
to the pub, to see your mortgage
adviser or to a work tribunal

Insist on climbing into the supermarket trolley when out shopping with your partner

HOW TO PARTY YOUNGER

Instead of arriving at 7.00 and leaving at 10.00, arrive at 10.00 and leave at 7.00

Spend all night playing with balloons and tooting away on a party blower, even when you've been invited to a polite dinner party

Turn the music up to full blast – these days it's the only way you can hear anything clearly

DOs AND DON'Ts FOR OLDER PEOPLE TRYING TO APPEAR YOUNG

DO	DON'T
Try anti-wrinkle cream	Don't smother your entire body in it
Try to keep up with fashion	Don't attempt a new career as a catwalk supermodel
Exercise regularly to keep yourself fit and healthy	Exercise too strenuously, or, ironically, this may put you in hospital
Get a nice even all-over tan	Overdo it and end up looking like a shrivelled and ancient piece of leather

THINGS YOU ALREADY HAVE IN COMMON WITH YOUNG PEOPLE

You probably never get properly dressed before noon

You let middle-aged people do all your fetching and carrying for you

You feel yourself to be surrounded by idiots

THINGS IT'S NEVER
TOO LATE TO DO

Travel the world – though it all may look a
bit blurrier than if you'd done it earlier

Find your real self – OK, it may be buried a
little deeper than it was a few years ago

Work out what you really want
to do in life while you are still
capable of doing anything!

Form a rock band – let's face it, there are a few septuagenarian ones out there already

GROWN-UP AND LESS-GROWN-UP WAYS TO BEHAVE AT WORK

GROWN-UP	LESS-GROWN-UP
Dress smartly	Have a special selection of animal onesies just for work
Have a business-like telephone voice for answering calls	Have a selection of comedy voices and silly accents to keep your boredom levels down
Always speak to clients with friendliness and respect	Greet them with the words, "What do you want this time?"
Whenever your boss asks you to help with something, carry out the task to the very best of your ability	Stand with your lip curled while telling them, "Why the heck would I want to do that?!"

HOW TO HOLIDAY YOUNGER

Ignore all the cultural sites and try to beat
your previous holiday alcohol intake

Instead of visiting castles, build
them on the beach

Enjoy buying up as many tacky
souvenirs as you can

Throw some shapes on the dance floor – even if some of them are the shapes of a person suffering from a bad back

KEEPING UP WITH MODERN TECHNOLOGY

Remember, Bluetooth wasn't a character from *Pirates of the Caribbean*

Blockchain is not some sort of mechanical device that will help unclog your toilet

Whenever you ask your partner to do something, try to avoid beginning your request by accidentally calling them "Siri"

FUN GAMES TO PLAY WHEN ENCOUNTERING OTHER OLD PEOPLE

Trying to outdo each other with tales of waiting times for hospital appointments

Making them think you're really young by boasting about all the social media platforms you're on

Helping them cross the road, carrying their shopping and generally acting as though you are their youthful carer

GROWN-UP AND LESS-GROWN-UP WAYS TO BEHAVE AT NIGHTCLUBS

GROWN-UP	LESS-GROWN-UP
Wear something age-appropriate but still fashionable	Wear the appropriate outfit for doing the "funky chicken"
Let your hair down, but act sensibly	Let your friends down by acting outrageously
Dance in a way that provides aerobic exercise and so strengthens your body	Dance in such a way that it leaves you unable to walk while at the same time damaging the fabric of surrounding buildings
Drink only in moderation	Get through more shots in one evening than a machine gun

FUN GAMES TO PLAY WHEN ENCOUNTERING YOUNGER PEOPLE

See how long it takes to annoy them with your non-politically-correct views on the issues of the day

Try to shock them with your memories of what you were doing at their age

Terrify them by tricking them into thinking that you might be their birth father or mother

Thrill them with completely fictitious stories about your meetings with everyone from Elvis to Che Guevara

APPROPRIATE AND INAPPROPRIATE CLOTHES

APPROPRIATE	INAPPROPRIATE
Clothes that fit your fuller figure	The jeans that you might have worn at 18, but which now have more of you hanging outside than inside
A classic, well-cut suit	Your birthday suit. No one wants to see that – even on the beach
A nice smart outfit that will make you feel strong and confident	A Superman or Wonder Woman costume
Something that fits loosely and makes you feel comfortable	Something that fits so loosely it makes those around you feel uncomfortable

EXERCISE FOR THE OLDER PERSON

Running – a bath

Jogging – your memory

Push-ups – to try to lift bits of your body
back towards where they should be

Chin-ups – particularly
good exercise if you now
have more than one chin

THINGS THAT TAKE UP SPACE IN THE HOMES OF AGEING NON-GROWN-UPS

- The skateboard, pogo stick and rollerskates you never quite mastered but thought you might one day get back to

- The flares, bomber jackets and big-shouldered jackets you are hoping will come back into fashion

- Your vinyl, CD, cassette, video, Betamax, DVD and LaserDisc collections

- Your book collection, which you always like to appear in front of during Zoom calls

- Old toys and worthless memorabilia – largely bought off eBay over the last 15 years

YOUR NEW
PHILOSOPHY

Online, no one knows how old you are

Most of your favourite actors and
rock stars are even older than you,
so they make you feel young

You've reached the peak of your
maturity and now you're coming
down the other side

GROWN-UP AND LESS-GROWN-UP WAYS TO BEHAVE AT THE DOCTOR'S

GROWN-UP	LESS-GROWN-UP
When asked, describe the symptoms	When asked, pretend to mishear and describe *The Simpsons*
Strip off when required	Strip off in the waiting room to save time
Do not get embarrassed if the doctor has to examine the more intimate areas of your body	Wobble your intimate areas around in front of the doctor while humming the song "Pour Some Sugar on Me"
Take any prescriptions or advice given to you by the doctor	Refuse to leave until the doctor gives you a sticker and a lollipop

WAYS TO HAVE FUN WITH THE ODD NOISES YOUR BODY MAY START TO MAKE

Record your creaking joints, add a bit of synthesizer, and have a big dance hit with it

Conceal a playback device about your person and have a riveting selection of different sounds that you can emit when getting in and out of soft furnishings (Swanee whistles, duck quacks, echoing screams, etc.)

Whenever your knees crack, convince your partner that it was actually someone knocking on the door

Gather friends and family around to treat them to a live performance of the noises your tummy makes after a large meal

KEEPING UP WITH
MODERN MUSIC

If you like it and it's got a tune, it's probably completely out of date

If your first reaction is to switch it off, it's probably cutting-edge stuff you should be pretending to like

If you hear a tune you actually recognize, don't get too excited – it will probably be a sample in the middle of something else

CLOTHES YOU MUST STOP WEARING

Any sportswear featuring a logo for a
brand that went out of business
prior to the millennium

Anything you have been waiting more
than 10 years to come back into fashion

Anything in beige that will over time
make you look like a fading sepia
image of yourself

Absolutely everything you own all at the same time as part of a desperate effort to keep warm

THINGS THAT WILL MAKE YOU LOOK YOUNG AND THINGS THAT WILL MAKE YOU LOOK TOO YOUNG

YOUNG	TOO YOUNG
Swimming with dolphins	Swimming with water wings
Watching *Friends*	Talking to imaginary friends
Playing hip hop	Playing hopscotch
Driving around town in your first car	Driving around town in your pedal car

THINGS YOU SHOULDN'T BE DOING

Screwing your face up every time
you try to read something

Making noises when getting out of a chair
(creaking noises can't be helped though)

Telling everyone that things
were better in your day

DRINKS THAT ONLY OLD PEOPLE HAVE

Port and lemon

Gin and It

Cocoa made with actual cocoa

Dandelion and burdock, and any
other drinks made from weeds
from the back garden

WAYS YOU CAN BLEND IN WITH YOUNGER PEOPLE

Tell them the reason for your pale and greying appearance is that you're a goth

Go to very badly lit nightclubs

Find a group of younger people who are also putting on a bit of weight on and/or beginning to lose their hair

A hoodie and shades can hide
a multitude of sins

THE ADVANTAGES AND DISADVANTAGES OF BEING A GRANDPARENT

ADVANTAGES	DISADVANTAGES
You get to play with toys again	The instructions are printed too small
You get a second childhood	You'll still be in it when they grow out of their first one
You get to share all your grandchildren's sweets	Unlike them, you're unlikely to grow another set of teeth
You get to go into the play park again	People disapprove if you start playing on any of the equipment

WAYS TO HAVE FUN WITH THE CHANGES IN YOUR APPEARANCE AS YOU AGE

Paint your laughter lines blue so they look like trendy tattoos

Get people to play "join the dots" on the liver spots on your hands

Convince people you're not moving slower than you used to – you're just performing t'ai chi

Any increases in the size of your nose and ears will provide you with extra space to get multiple piercings

AN OLDER PERSON'S GUIDE TO MODERN PHRASES

Cool – doesn't mean immediately
turning the heating up

YOLO – no, it's not some sort of
round toy on a string that is capable
of going particularly low

Netflix and chill – this does not refer to
watching a nature documentary about
the Antarctic via a streaming service

WAYS TO KEEP UP WITH MODERN FOOD

A Whopper is not something you tell the
speed cops when you get pulled over

Bubble tea is not the name for
the noises your tummy makes after
you've drunk too many cuppas

Avocados are very trendy – but not as the
colour for your bathroom suite

YOUR DAILY ROUTINE AS AN AGEING NON-GROWN-UP

9.00 a.m. – animal-shaped breakfast
cereal and kids' TV

11.00 a.m. – skateboarding in the park

12.00 p.m. – cleaning up cuts
and bruises

1.00 p.m. – smiley-face potato pieces
and tomato sauce

2.00 p.m. – trying to beat your best
ever *Minecraft* score

3.00 p.m. – telling everyone on social
media you've just beaten
your *Minecraft* score

11.00 p.m. – bedtime!

NIGHTCLUBS THEY SHOULD HAVE FOR OLDER PEOPLE

Studio 94

Hamstringfellows

The Croakercabana

The Ministry of Please Would You Keep the Sound Down to an Acceptable Level

THINGS THAT TAKE UP SPACE IN THE BRAINS OF AGEING NON-GROWN-UPS

- If I throw an all-night party, is it absolutely necessary for it to go on all night?

- Will people notice I'm wearing knee supports when I do my high-energy disco dancing?

- Will I look younger if I vape?

- Should I try to learn to text using only one hand?

- Can I stay warm while still looking cool?

- Who *did* put the "ram" in the "ramalamadingdong"? And why?

HOW TO DRIVE YOUNGER

Avoid having a packet of mints
on the dashboard

Practise doing handbrake turns –
or perhaps in your case, handbrake
three-point turns to avoid too
much damage to your car

Show off your vehicle by driving up
and down the main street – without
making it look like you're lost and
looking for your turning

Try to go more than 20 mph
occasionally – especially
on motorways

WAYS TO FOOL EVERYONE INTO THINKING YOU'RE COOL

WHAT THEY THINK YOU'RE DOING	WHAT YOU'RE REALLY DOING
Listening to music on your earphones	Listening to a radio gardening programme
Going into a trendy boutique to buy clothes	Going in to complain about the volume of their music
A high-intensity dance workout	Trying to get rid of pins and needles because your leg has just gone to sleep
Checking your social media on your snazzy new phone	Looking up the instructions to see how to use your snazzy new phone

THINGS YOU HAVE IN COMMON WITH TEENAGERS

Given half a chance, you'll sleep till lunchtime

You both find middle-aged people annoying – to teenagers because they're too old, and to you because they're too young

You probably both wish more people wanted to have sex with you

MODERN PLACE NAMES YOU NEED TO KEEP UP WITH

Bombay is now Mumbai –
unless you're ordering Bombay
potatoes in an Indian restaurant

And Peking is Beijing – unless
you're buying a Pekingese dog.
It's all so confusing, isn't it?

The Czech Republic that was part of
Czechoslovakia is now Czechia – so it's
always worth a quick "czech" to make
sure it hasn't changed again

HOW TO KEEP THE YEARS AT BAY

Ban birthdays – be like Winnie the Pooh
and have "un-birthdays" instead

As your eyesight gets worse, you will look
younger in the mirror, so ditch those specs!

Always remember it's best to keep
moving – your ageing joints will surely
come round to the idea in the end

Remember to always eat lots
of ultra-healthy food – followed
by plenty of cake and alcohol
to try to get rid of the taste

KEEPING UP WITH MODERN COMEDY

Everything you used to laugh at
is not allowed any more, and all
the words that used to be bleeped
out now seem to be bleeped in

Even the youngest comedians today
don't seem to bother telling many
"knock knock" jokes

As a basic rule of thumb, all comedians
who you've never heard of are brilliant
and innovative, and all those that you have
heard of are sell-outs who are no longer
as good as they used to be

THINGS TO BAN FROM YOUR HOUSE IF YOU WANT TO SEEM YOUNGER

That proper teapot

Those doilies you get out
for special occasions

Any printed-out photographs of yourself
that provide evidence that you reached
adulthood in the pre-digital-camera era

Any music- or video-playing
equipment that requires
physical discs or tapes

LESSONS TO LEARN FROM YOUNG PEOPLE

If you act like tomorrow will never come, you will stay the same age forever!

You only live once – so you may as well do the fun bits of life as many times as you can

Their natural inclination is to rebel against the older generation – so yours can be to rebel against yourself

YOUTHFUL PURSUITS WHERE AGE IS NOT A BARRIER

Hanging around on street corners,
making a noise and being a nuisance

Creating a trendy young-sounding new
online identity for yourself – although
you may then immediately forget your
password to access it

Making exciting 60-second-long TikTok
videos of yourself – you may of course
have to speed the film up to do what you
wanted in just 60 seconds

Computer games – though the excitement could be a bit much at your age

GROWN-UP AND LESS-GROWN-UP WAYS TO BEHAVE AT ROCK CONCERTS

GROWN-UP	LESS-GROWN-UP
Sing along to your favourite numbers	Jump on stage, shove the singer out of the way and belt 'em out yourself
Buy a souvenir T-shirt	Rip out and take home a souvenir seat
Stand swaying with your arm up in the air holding a lighter	Stand swaying with your arm up in the air holding your underwear
Filming a few moments on your phone to remember the evening	Spending the whole evening talking loudly to someone on your phone so you end up missing the whole show

WAYS YOU ARE ALREADY FOOLING THE REST OF THE WORLD

You don't actually listen to half the modern songs on your Spotify playlist – you play your trusty old CDs and vinyl in private instead

You're on social media despite being completely antisocial in real life

You have bought yourself a Linguaphone course to teach you how to speak in young people's slang

Your profile picture
was taken in 1972

WAYS TO TAKE UP A ROCK 'N' ROLL LIFESTYLE IN YOUR LATER YEARS

Wearing black leather pyjamas
and slippers

Trashing your hotel room when on
holiday in the Lake District

Taking lots of drugs – OK, in your case
these will probably be vitamin tablets
and/or prescriptions from your doctor

THINGS YOU CAN HAVE TANTRUMS ABOUT AS YOU GET OLDER

Your partner trying to stop you eating
and drinking what you want

Being bossed about by petty officials who
are younger than you are

Any unexpected scratch, dent or penalty
charge that befalls your car

When you find you've not been given all the loyalty points you're due at your local supermarket

GROWN-UP AND LESS-GROWN-UP WAYS TO BEHAVE WITH MONEY

GROWN-UP	LESS-GROWN-UP
Give some to charity	Write to all the old-age charities asking when you're going to get your share
Put some in a savings account	Empty all your savings accounts and buy a mid-life-crisis sports car
Put some money aside for your old age	Blow all your cash on experiences likely to make you feel prematurely aged
Invest your money in funds to help conserve and protect the planet for future generations	Spend all your money on so much booze your pickled body will be marvelled over by future generations

THINGS YOU'RE FREE TO DO NOW YOU'RE OLDER

Say what you think – whether
people like it or not

Give regular updates on the declining state
of your body to anyone who will listen

Become a lovable twinkly-eyed older
person simply by being enthusiastic
about modern things and not constantly
complaining about the declining
state of your body

Having achieved maturity
you are now free to have fun by
behaving like a small child again!

Have you enjoyed this book? If so, find us on Facebook at **Summersdale Publishers**, on Twitter at **@Summersdale** and on Instagram at **@summersdalebooks** and get in touch. We'd love to hear from you!

www.summersdale.com